HEADWAY LIFEGUID

ALEXANDER TECHNIQUE

Glynn Macdonald

Frederick Matthias Alexander (1869–1955)

'Nature is full of miracles'
F.M. Alexander

HEADWAY LIFEGUIDES

ALEXANDER TECHNIQUE

Glynn Macdonald

Headway • Hodder & Stoughton

I would like to thank the following people for their help and encouragement: Reverend Raymond Avent, Anne Battye, David Birch, Michael Bloch, George J.D. Bruce, David Carey, Walter Carrington, Dilys Carrington, Penny Cherns, Teresa Chris, Martin Creese, Roger Croucher, Mr Garfield Davies, Doris Dietschy, Jean M.O. Fischer, Michael Fredericks, Rowena Gaunt, Sue Hart, John Jayne, Professor Brian Ketterer, David Levitt, Joe Links, Tony Loyd, Mary Lutyens, The Very Reverend Michael Mayne, Alison Mayne, Ron MacDonald, June MacDonald, John E. Macdonald, Antonio Moreno, Dr Peter Nixon, Maysoon Pachachi, Anna Pallant, Clarissa Palmer, Dr Michael Pokorny, Jan Sargent, Jayne Saunderson, Christine Shewell, Dr Stuart Unger, Elisabeth Walker, Gilly White, Peggy Williams, Giselle Wolf and Helen Wynter.

With special thanks to Sally and Nicola, Miriam and Dylan, Ruth and Rico and to Angie Herzberg who took the photographs. And last but not least, my wonderful family, Robert, Jessi and Jack, who made it all possible.

The author and publishers would like to thank Christina Jansen for the cover photograph, Roddy Paine for the commissioned photographs, Science Photo Library for the photograph on page 25, J. Allan Cash for the photograph on page 28, Taurus Graphics for the drawing on page 29 and Annabel Milne for the drawings on pages 12, 16, 17, 18, 26, 56, 58 and 59.

Cataloguing in Publication Data is available from the British Library

ISBN 0 340 59680 5

First published 1994
Impression number 10   9   8   7   6   5   4   3   2   1
Year   1988   1997   1996   1995   1994

Typeset by Wearset, Boldon, Tyne and Wear.
Printed in Great Britain for Hodder & Stoughton Educational, a division of Hodder Headline Plc, Mill Road, Dunton Green, Sevenoaks, Kent TN13 2YA by Thomson Litho Ltd, East Kilbride.

CONTENTS

INTRODUCTION

What is the Alexander Technique?

Most of us would like to change some things about ourselves. It may be our voice, our quick temper, our posture or our lack of confidence. We feel there must be an easier way of living but we do not know how to find it.

The Alexander Technique is about learning *how* to change. It is not a magic formula but a careful method of learning about our mind and body so that we can begin to eradicate the faults and habits that are holding us back. Over the years, the Alexander Technique has helped people to change for the better. We can begin to watch how we stand, walk, speak, sit, work at our desk or at the kitchen sink. We can observe how we deal with our children, parents, partners and friends; with success, failure, disappointment, anxiety, competition and fatigue. We can change ourselves and learn how to work as a unit so that we can have more time and space. We can gain the freedom of choosing how we operate, both within ourselves and in the outside world. The Alexander Technique is about making life easier by working *with* our mind and body, not struggling against them.

One of the problems we face when we want to change is the size of the task. 'Where do I start?' is a familiar cry. If we bought a new appliance, such as a vacuum cleaner or a computer, we would start by reading the instructions, the 'Directions for Use', *before* we began using it. These instructions would have told us what to do to get the best out of the appliance and, even more importantly, what *not* to do. The Alexander Technique provides 'Directions for Use' for each of us. There are certain things which will help us get more out of ourselves and there are certain things we should not do. We are talking about improving the way we use ourselves to maximise our potential and avoid unnecessary and sometimes harmful procedures which go against the Manufacturer's Instructions.

Why is it called the Alexander Technique? F.M. Alexander is the name of the man who formulated this way of working. The definition of a technique is 'a means of achieving one's purpose'. So the Alexander Technique is the means of achieving one's purpose in relation to finding a better way of using oneself. We are not used to thinking about 'using' ourselves. We understand using the vacuum cleaner and using the computer, but we can use ourselves to lead to an easier way of living and when this happens we can get more out of life *and have a good time*.

The history of F.M. Alexander and his work

F.M. Alexander was born in Australia in 1869. That same year saw the birth of Mahatma Gandhi, Edwin Lutyens the architect and Henri Matisse the French Impressionist, and the opening of the Suez Canal. Life was so different 120 years ago, pre-Darwin, pre-Freud, pre-television.

At that time life in Australia was wild and hard. Alexander was born in a lonely outpost in Tasmania where to survive at all you had to keep your wits about you and cope with whatever problems arose. Strong-willed and talented, Alexander came out of the 'Bush' and began a career as a Shakespearean actor. In 1895 a New Zealand newspaper recognised 'his splendid voice, remarkable for its resonance and power and sympathy which he used with great taste'. He was enjoying success and looked poised for a fine career when he began to have difficulties with his voice. To his annoyance, he had developed the habit of sniffing and gasping and by the end of a performance he would be hoarse, unable to make any sound at all.

Doctors could find nothing organically wrong with him and suggested that he should rest and simply wait for his voice to return. Alexander was not satisfied with this suggestion. He wanted to know why he lost his voice and why it would return if he did not speak. He decided it must be something he was 'doing' that caused the problem. Patiently, he began to observe himself each time he came to speak to try to discover if he was doing something wrong. To this end he set up a series of mirrors in which he could see his front and side view simultaneously and so began his long road of self-discovery.

Slowly he began to realise that each time he came to speak he would begin a series of habits which interfered with the necessary freedom in his voice. He observed that he tightened the muscles at the back of his neck, collapsed his head back and down on his neck and became shorter in stature. As he did this he noticed that he contracted his shoulders and his face and jaw stiffened. He was surprised that he could have been unconscious of all these habits for so long. He did not want to create these tensions, yet they happened in spite of his wishes. He knew he had to stop these interferences before he came to speak. He saw how important posture and the correct alignment of his head on his neck and spine were. If he allowed his head to collapse backwards and his chest to collapse downwards, he had no hope of producing the strong, clear voice he wanted.

Over a long period of time he became able to stop these old harmful habits and his voice returned stronger than ever. He discovered that his breathing improved and his whole body became generally fitter and stronger. From his practical experience with its beneficial side-effects he formulated the Alexander Technique.

He opened an Academy for Voice Studies in Sydney and began to teach his technique. As his success with voice teaching grew, people realised that his work made dramatic improvements to their posture and breathing. He became known as the 'breathing man' and the popularity of his work spread beyond voice specialists, such as actors and singers, to people in all walks of life.

In 1904 he was invited to London to present his work. Alexander thought the Londoners were in poor shape. The Australian poet 'Banjo' Patterson described it well:

> 66 *And the hurrying people daunt me, and their pallid faces haunt me.*
> *As they shoulder one another in their rush and nervous haste*
> *With their eager eyes and greedy, and their stunted forms and weedy*
> *For townsfolk have no time to grow, they have no time to waste.* 99

For the next 50 years, F.M. worked with the same patience and skill which he had shown in his initial experiment on himself and helped others to discover a better way of being. He wrote four books: *Man's Supreme Inheritance, The Use of the Self, Constructive Conscious Control of the Individual* and *The Universal Constant in Living.* Their titles tell of his breadth of vision and the great legacy he has left. The week before he died he was working full time – he was in his 86th year.

F.M. Alexander on his eightieth birthday, with the Earl of Lytton

The Alexander Technique today

Alexander died in 1955; that same year saw the death of Albert Einstein. Einstein changed the way we think about the universe; Alexander changed the way we think about ourselves. He started his school for training teachers in 1932 with six students. Today the Alexander Technique has over 1000 teachers worldwide with 500 students undergoing a full-time three-year training course programme. Alexander teachers are employed in all the major drama and music colleges in the UK – the London Academy of Music and Dramatic Art, the Royal Academy of Dramatic Art, the Guildhall School of Music and Drama, the Royal National Theatre, the Central School of Speech and Drama, Guildford Drama School, Mountview Theatre School, the Royal Academy of Music, the Royal College of Music, the Royal Northern College of Music and the Purcell School. Some primary and secondary schools have Alexander Technique teachers and this area of self-education is of great interest. If we can help our children to take better care of themselves and make better use of their time, we may look forward to a more balanced and happier future.

Alexander teachers are committed professionals who belong to official societies with published Codes of Ethics. Guidelines for training are observed and carefully monitored. Addresses of societies who will supply a comprehensive list of teachers are given at the end of the book.

The process of change is not easy but with knowledge, patience and perseverance we can develop an easier way of working with fewer knee-jerk reactions. As we follow the Technique's 'Directions' our attitude to life may become more carefree and lighter. We have the possibility of less pain and the chance of helping ourselves avoid unnecessary strain and effort. The stress of life does not go away but we can learn how to deal more efficiently with it. We are in safe hands with the Alexander Technique as it works with nature, not against it.

1

HOW THE MIND AND BODY WORK

The breath of life

Have you ever stopped to think about your breathing? It is such a basic part of you that you tend to forget about it, but without that vital function going on continuously, not much else can happen in your mind and body. If you stop breathing, something is wrong. You may feel dizzy, you may faint, your heart may stop, you may die. It is a simple and essential fact – Breath is Life.

The process of breathing is called 'respiration' and it happens at an autonomic level; that means that without any direct help from us, the function of breathing continues. It is regulated to provide oxygen to all the cells of the body and to remove carbon dioxide from them. Although this process *is* going on all the time, often it is not working as efficiently as it could. This can lead to feelings of tiredness and a general lack of energy. The cells of your body may not be getting enough oxygen and there can be an excess of carbon dioxide present. Your lungs become like a stuffy room with all the windows shut. Breathing should ventilate every corner of the room.

Conversely, we tend to overbreathe in the upper chest, which requires great effort and furnishes us with a comparatively small amount of air. We need to repeat the inbreath too frequently to get sufficient air. This is called 'hyperventilation' and means that air is being circulated, but only in the top half of the lungs. Think of the room again and imagine that only the air near the ceiling is moving and the air in the lower half of the room is stagnant. Hyperventilation lowers the amount of carbon dioxide in the blood and increases its acidity. These changes cause a wide variety of symptoms which include dizziness, feelings of unreality, pins and needles, choking and chest pain. When chest pain occurs, anxiety builds and can lead to the fear of heart attack.

The problem of overbreathing and the habit of underbreathing are fairly common. The Alexander Technique addresses these problems in a very direct way. The instruction is simple – 'Breathe out!'.

We have an ingrained belief that it is important to breathe in or 'take a good deep breath'. What we have to learn to do is get the air out to increase the volume of the chest cavity and create a decrease in pressure which in turn allows air to rush into the lungs.

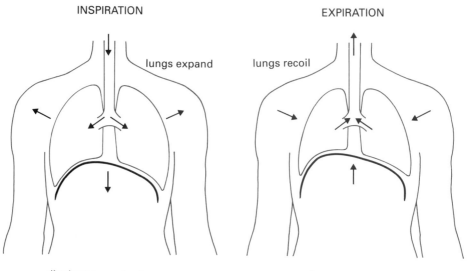

The mechanics of breathing

When babies are born the first movement the lungs make is to expel the fluid in them and clear the passages so that air can rush in. The first breath enlivens them, their colour changes and they can make their first sound.

The body is not a solid structure but is made up of spaces and cavities. The lungs are a vivid example of hundreds of branch-like spaces constantly being ventilated by our breath.

However, we tend to limit this function of respiration. We can see the first signs of this in growing babies. They begin to hold their breath, often preceded by a bout of crying, until they can turn nearly blue from a lack of oxygen.

When the child begins school, the instruction is given, 'Take a breath and . . .'. The idea of needing to take a breath is not helpful. It is one of the things in our Directions for Use which we should not do. The school concert where pupils have been told 'Take a breath and sing' is a good example of faulty breathing at work – children puffed up with air, grim faces, hands clenched, feeling they have insufficient air to get to the end of the song.

We often feel we do not have enough air for the task in hand. Usually we try to remedy this by gasping air in through the mouth, which is not a good idea, as dirty, dry and often cold air comes directly into the throat and then into the lungs. Air should be filtered, moistened and warmed before it enters the lungs and this happens very effectively when we use our nose for breathing. So the second Direction for Use to follow is 'Breathe through the nose'. What we should not do is gasp air in through

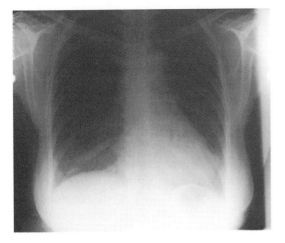

X-rays of the lungs:
(a) poor posture;

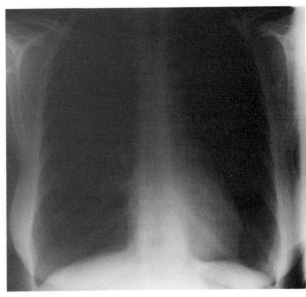

(b) good posture

the mouth. We have got into the habit of mouth breathing – often it has happened when our nose has been blocked through a cold, but when the cold has passed we should not keep taking in air through the wrong way.

Directions for Use

- Remember to breathe out
- Do not take a breath and hold it
- Do not breathe only in the upper part of the chest
- Do not breathe in through the mouth
- Breathe in through the nose

How posture and efficient breathing are related

If your lungs are going to be able to empty and refill efficiently you need to give them enough space. The lungs are two sacs contained in the ribcage which has 12 pairs of fixed ribs and two pairs of floating ribs which are attached only at the back and are free in front. If you are collapsed in the back and slumped down in front, then the ribs push down and squeeze on the lungs. The ribs are designed for protection and strength, but they also have the potential for easy, springy movement. This springiness is only possible if they have a good structure supporting them and allowing them to be free. The head correctly balanced on the neck and spine can give the necessary structural support and encourages better co-ordination.

The Alexander Technique is about learning how this relationship of the head, neck and back works to maximise the body's potential. Alexander considered this postural understanding so important he called it 'The Primary Control'. 'Primary' means 'earliest, chief or most important'. 'Control' means 'the power of directing or commanding', so this 'chief command' is the most important part of our Directions for Use. Without an understanding of how this relationship works, we are limiting our whole physical potential, so let us look at how this Primary Control operates.

In all vertebrates, that is, animals with backbones, and that includes us, the position of the head is very important. Where the head leads, the

Four-legged animal: direction of head is the same as direction of movement – both forward

body will follow. It is like the engine of the train with the carriages following. The four-legged animals have it easier than us as the direction of their head and back follows the same direction as their line of movement.

When it comes to human beings, this becomes more complicated. The principle is the same – where the head leads the body follows – but when we stood up the line of movement changed. We move forward but the direction along the spine has to continue up through the head.

Two-legged animal: direction of head is up; direction of movement is forward

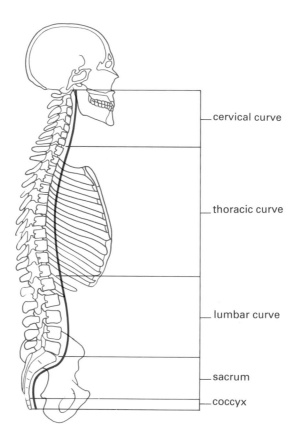

cervical curve

thoracic curve

lumbar curve

sacrum

coccyx

The head and spinal column

The head is delicately balanced on the backbone, which is a column of vertebrae and discs. The head is a heavy mass weighing between eight and fifteen pounds with the ability to nod freely forward in a subtle, gentle movement. It is not meant to be fixed stiffly on to the spine, but often the neck muscles are so tight that this very important releasing movement cannot happen. A lot of distress in the form of headaches, shoulder and back pain is caused by the restriction of movement in the relationship between the head and neck. Alexander had seen this problem in himself when he noticed the way he collapsed and tightened his neck as he came to speak.

The ability to allow this gentle nod forward to happen will increase with practice and you may notice that with the nod operating you can take the pressure off the muscles at the back of the neck. If they release and begin to stretch and lengthen we feel a weight lifted off us and begin to experience a sense of lightness and well-being. We can begin to appreciate gravity rather than being pushed down by it. Gravity works to keep us on the planet; it is an essential force, but if we are stiff and pulled down, then gravity becomes just another 'weight on our mind'.

In order to get the benefit of being light and springy, we have to stop tightening and collapsing, by allowing the head and all the joints of the body to work more freely. Every bone in the body* forms a joint with some other bone. Without joints we could make no movements at all, our bodies would be rigid and immobile. The joints are designed to release and expand, but often we hinder this ability by becoming rigid and inflexible and pain can result.

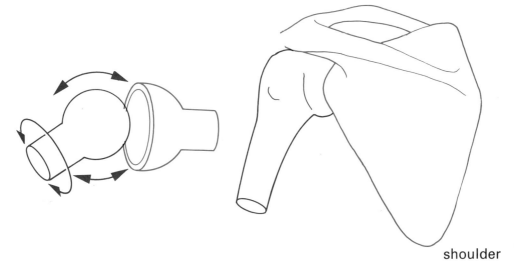

shoulder

Ball and socket joint (shoulder, hip): permits the widest range of movement

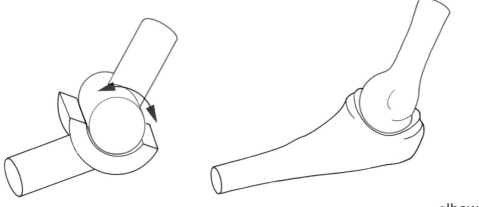

elbow

Hinge joint (elbow, knee): permits movement in only two directions (flexion and extension)

---

* Except one: the hyoid bone does not join to another bone; the tongue anchors to it.

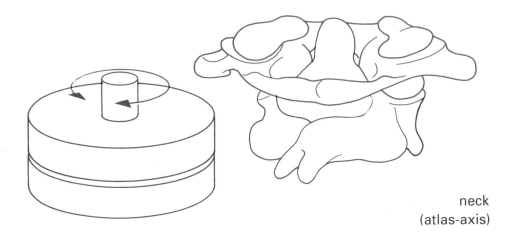

neck
(atlas-axis)

Pivot joint (atlas–axis in the neck): permits pivot movement

If we think of young children we see the pattern working beautifully. They are light, springy and inexhaustible compared to the stick men we have become. So keeping this freedom in the neck joint and allowing the head to go up and lengthen along the spine is vital. This new understanding of postural structure allows the rib cage to operate freely on the principle of release. This encourages the ribs to widen and the lungs to fill more completely. We get more oxygen and therefore more energy and as we stop pushing down on our joints we become more mobile and less stiff.

It is important to remember that we need to think before each action. Perhaps we worry that it will take too much time or limit our spontaneity. This is not true, for as we learn to apply our Directions for Use to each activity, everyday actions begin to require less effort and we put ourselves under less strain. We begin to understand the saying, 'More haste, less speed'. If we rush on thoughtlessly, we may get less done and make more mistakes.

Directions for Use

- Do not stiffen your neck
- Do not pull your head back
- Let the head nod gently forward
- Do not slump down in front
- Do not tighten the joints

Learning how to stop

> 66 *If we will stop doing the wrong thing, the right thing does itself.* 99
>
> F.M. Alexander

Learning to stop is an essential part of the Alexander Technique. However, the practice of stopping is not permanent – we are learning to stop in order to go. It is similar to driving your car up to a set of traffic lights. You are expected to stop if the light is red. You will not be stationary for long, but you *must* stop. If you do not stop there will be chaos at the lights. The red-light rule is one that you should obey. The need to obey this rule of stopping also exists in the Directions for Use for your mind and body. If this process of stopping – known as 'inhibition' or 'saying "No"' – is not working, then unwanted and unnecessary movements are happening all the time. The inhibitory process blocks out all the irrelevant messages so that one clear action can happen. If this did not happen there would be chaos – like a telephone switchboard jammed with calls and no possibility of a single line.

All the patterns we need for normal functioning are laid down in the human mind and body like a wonderful map. Some of the paths on this map have been covered up by years of bad habits and general misuse. The paths need clearing, so that the way can be rediscovered. When we begin to learn about stopping, the body has a chance to operate according to its design. We have become used to reacting quickly and subconsciously to any idea that comes to us. We do not give ourselves time to consider *how* we are going to proceed. The aim of 'inhibition' in the Alexander Technique is to prevent, or hold in check, the wrong response. Let us take the example of people who need speech lessons. Often the problem is the simple tendency of failing to pause between sentences, so that all the words come tumbling out on top of each other. When you suggest that they should stop between sentences to break this habit they feel that their speech may become too slow. In fact, quite the reverse happens; their speech becomes more audible and easier to comprehend and they stop sniffing and gasping air in to breathe. Sometimes singers feel that if they pause they cannot keep time in their songs but once again, the pause required for inhibition is only momentary and results in much freer expression.

It is interesting to watch an animal employing this process of inhibition. When you see a cat stalking a bird, consider how it stops, its attention held by its prey, slowly creeps forward, stops again, moves, stops, then pounces like an uncoiled spring, releasing enormous energy. The ability to stop before each movement is an essential part of the exercise.

So before these new patterns of mind and body can be utilised, you have to stop the old reactions. The instruction 'Take your time' is very helpful in realising how pointless it is to keep rushing on, giving no thought to *how* you are proceeding. The little bit of time that it takes to stop before going on will help prevent your wasting energy. It is not a long stop, just a momentary pause before the next action.

The physiologist Benjamin Libet's research suggests that our behaviour is being initiated by unconscious cerebral processes prior to conscious intention. That means that we are preparing to act even before we are aware of choosing to do so. In this way, actions tend to get carried out, whether we have chosen them or not. However, he found that there was a short period of time between the unconscious preparation and the actual execution of the movement during which a person becomes aware of getting ready to act and can make a conscious choice; either to carry out the action or not. The potential to inhibit response, that is stopping what we do not want to happen, is vital in making conscious choices.

Directions for Use

- Stop before you go
- Breathe out
- Do not work directly for the end
- Refuse to respond too quickly

Think before you act

As we become more conscious of the way the mind and body work together, we begin to understand that being able to change the way we think changes the way we are. The system has been laid down by nature.

A signal from the brain comes before every action, no matter how simple or seemingly easy that action appears. If our nose is itchy, we scratch it. We have a whole programme of internal messages that make this possible. Nerves carry these messages, or instructions, to the individual muscles, which are bunched together in bundles and tied into the next muscle group. The messages come down like a shower of rain – first a few drops, then some more, then a real downpour which eases off and finally stops. Each tiny muscle fibre, like each rain drop, makes up the whole.

The response is immediate and a concerted effort. The body is the orchestra and the mind is the conductor. It is the job of the conductor to direct the orchestra just as it is the job of the mind to direct the body. However, it is not a one-way process. The conductor gets feedback from the members of his orchestra which informs his choices. The mind gets feedback from the body and changes in choices may result. This body sense is called the 'kinaesthetic sense'. We have five senses which we all know: sight, touch, hearing, taste and smell. This sixth sense, which is less familiar to us, tells us where we are in time and space. It helps us do what we want to do and not just react in the same old harmful patterns to which we have become accustomed. There are some formalised thoughts or 'Directions' which the Alexander Technique provides to make this communication between the mind and body possible.

The first Direction is, 'Let the neck be free'. This thought gives the message to the muscles of the neck to stop holding on so tightly. The suboccipital muscles just below the skull are very good at tightening, so we have to remember not to give them any encouragement. They tend to over-tighten with very little reason and in some cases are permanently locked. As you unlock these muscles the natural nod of the head can happen. This movement takes the pressure off the spine so that it can lengthen and the head can go up.

The second Direction is, 'Let the head go forward and up'.

As these two commands are given, the body lengthens along the spine and the ribcage begins to expand so that the torso increases in size. From this feedback the next Direction comes: 'Let the back lengthen and widen'. As this happens the head can go up more as the neck remains free.

So these Directions facilitate the optimum peformance for us. The word 'performance' is often used for cars and machines. The performance of a machine or car can be measured in good conditions and in bad conditions. We can also measure performance in people; we are all performing – not just actors, singers, musicians and dancers. To perform means to carry into effect some task or function. Nikolas Tinbergen, who won the Nobel Prize for Physiology and Medicine in 1973, refers to this area of human performance:

> **66** *I recommend the Alexander Technique as an extremely sophisticated form of rehabilitation. Many types of underperformance and even ailments, both mental and physical, can be alleviated, sometimes to a surprising extent, by teaching the body musculature to function differently.* **99**

The expert guidance of an Alexander Technique teacher is invaluable. Through careful hand contact and verbal instruction the teacher can guide you gently through new sensory experiences. Alexander said, 'There is no such thing as a right position, but there is such a thing as a right direction'. When you go to a teacher you will get the benefit of years of experience that dealing with their own psycho-physical changes of 'mind and body' has given them. I recommend you to have a course of lessons with a teacher registered by the Society of Teachers of the Alexander Technique (STAT) who will have been carefully trained in the process of learning 'how to learn'.

Directions for Use

- Let the neck be free
- Let the head go forward and up
- Let the back lengthen and widen

An Alexander teacher and her pupil 'at work'

2

WORKING WITH NATURE

Ease and disease

When you are functioning well, all the things that you have to do in a day seem relatively easy. Those same tasks can become so very much more difficult when you do not feel well. Getting out of bed becomes a challenge and everything seems to get you down. If you compare this state with how you felt on holiday with the pressures off, time for yourself, your body exercised and fresh air in your lungs, you seemed like a different person. Life was easy and you felt on top of things. This easy living, which a holiday releases, could become more constant if we changed the way we operated by applying our 'Directions' and inhibitory procedure and allowing the natural spirals and reflexes to operate.

What are 'spirals' and how do they work? Think of throwing a ball or a discus. There is an upward twist in the whole body which allows the arm to come round and hurl the object. This spiral spring is important in nature. All plant growth, the movement of water in whirlpools and even the galaxies are in spiral patterns. It is the same in the human body; nothing is completely straight. All the bones, joints and muscle structures are spirally formed. Even the structure of the heart is built on this spiral pattern. When you watch someone curl up for a sleep, you can see the spirals working beautifully. Cats are expert at this. Conversely, when you watch someone getting themselves 'all in a twist', you can see the whole body pulling down into a whirlpool of tension.

Curled for comfort

Spiral galaxy in the constellation of Pisces

A whirlpool of tension

The release of the spirals is very important when we consider movement. Your body is designed to move and if you obey the pattern of spirals, you will move more easily and gracefully. Stiffness in the joints and muscles is often brought about by pulling down and not allowing the curving spirals to operate. In Chapter 3 you will find the section on Crawling helpful to experience the operation of the spirals in the cross pattern movement.

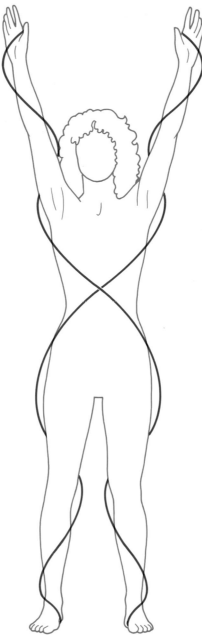

Spirals in the human body allow release

Spirals work in close association with the reflexes. A reflex action is an automatic response to nerve stimulation, like a sneeze. When a door slams, or the telephone rings, or someone shouts, or the dog barks, and you jump in response to the sudden noise, that is a reflex. When you say, 'I nearly jumped out of my skin', you are describing a very deep physiological fact.

Reflexes are very important and without them we would not function normally. The most basic reflex, the one that often saves our life, is called the 'startle pattern reflex'. We know this reflex very well and readily recognise it in ourselves and others. Think of what it was like when a friend who was watering the garden suddenly turned the hose on you. Your neck tightened, your shoulders went up to your ears, your legs stiffened, you held your breath and you hated your friend. When we lived in a less protected way, this startle pattern reflex was caused not by the threat of a drenching, but by the possibility of a very real danger in the form of a tiger, a snake, a spear or a witch doctor. In order to survive in the wild against predators much larger than us, we had to be able to make an instant decision whether to stay and fight or run away.

The startle pattern reflex always comes before the fight or flight response. It is a very useful reflex, but it should not be maintained longer than is necessary. Most of us hold it for too long: to respond with the reflex action is healthy, but to maintain it is neurotic. So next time the dog barks or the hose is pointed towards you, see how quickly you can make your decision to stop stiffening your neck.

When you stop stiffening your neck it becomes possible for all the other reflexes in the body to work. As you saw in Chapter 1, breathing is a reflex. So, you begin to build up a picture of yourself as a series of reflexes, all working freely together, bringing ease to every action. Remember yourself on holiday and how easy walking seemed. You could go on for hours with a 'spring in your step'. This elasticity in walking is made possible by the spring reflex, the motive power in movement.

Easy!

So in order to operate according to the Directions that nature intended, we have to understand and use these two important mechanisms: spirals and released reflexes. This will result in minimum effort and maximum efficiency. This pattern can be illustrated by Doctor Peter Nixon's Human Function Curve.

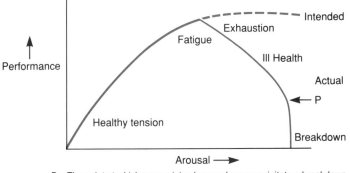

P – The point at which even minimal arousal may precipitate a breakdown

The Human Function Curve is a model illustrating the way we go over the top into exhaustion and deteriorating function if we allow ourselves to be aroused to make effort and struggle beyond the level of healthy fatigue. In exhaustion, our trying harder to overcome the deterioration makes us less efficient because our performance is already on a downward slope: the extra effort increases the arousal and carries us further downhill. Fighting to close the gap between what we actually can do and what we think is intended of us only widens it. High levels of arousal interferes with the restorative value of sleep and so aggravate the exhaustion.

This exhaustion, or lack of ease, is often the forerunner to disease. Medical science realises that the attitude of the patient plays a very important part in the recovery process. However, you can take control and positively re-establish the ease which you have lost.

Children – our hope for the future

Parents and teachers often ask what is the best age for children to begin Alexander Technique lessons. As we have seen, 'technique' is a means whereby you can achieve better use of yourself. Assuming that there have been no complications in the birth to have a negative effect, most babies are 'using' themselves very well, as nature intended. Their Directions are clear, their lung power is unrestricted, their reflexes are quick and appropriate and they have the ability to twist and turn in released spirals. Their energy seems to be unlimited as they explore themselves and their environment with never-ending interest.

Their will is strong and focused; they know what they want and they go for it. As long as they are loved, protected and nourished with food and fresh air, they grow at a remarkable pace, learning more in the first two years than in the whole of the rest of their lives.

By 'learning', I mean putting together all the experiences and sensations in a programme for living. Part of this programme has been put down before birth in a unique genetic code. A gene is a 'unit of heredity in a chromosome, controlling a particular inherited characteristic of an individual'. As parents we pass on patterns in the genes, ('the inheritance of nature') but we also pass on our patterns and habits of living, ('the inheritance of nurture'). If our own patterns of using our minds and bodies are poor, we will pass these bad habits on to our children.

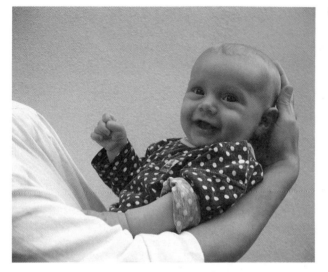

Giving good, early support

Setting a good example

It is reasonable to want to give our children the best possible start in life, and to do this it is important that we do not interfere unnecessarily in our babies' development. If we try to help them to walk or put them in mechanical baby walkers or in curved pushchairs, we could disturb the delicate balancing patterns that are being laid down in these early years.

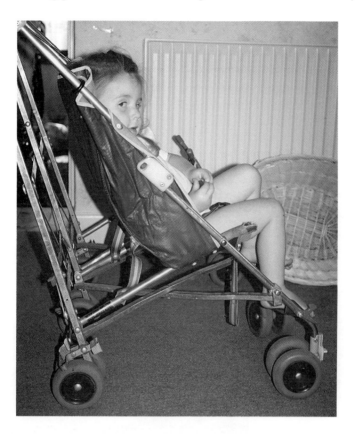

Babies will make the transition from each stage of development to the next quite naturally. It is tempting to offer the 'helping hand', but apart from keeping a watchful eye for danger, we can trust babies to 'find their own feet'. If we hurry their development they may skip vital stages. This is especially so in the important crawling phase. When we watch babies crawling we notice that the arm and leg on opposite sides of the body move simultaneously. When the left knee is moving forward, so is the right hand, and when the right knee is moving forward so is the left hand. The muscles move in diagonal connections across the body. An enormous amount of neurological feedback comes through the cross pattern reflex during this crawling time. The work of Doctors Dolman and Delcato in their studies with brain-damaged children provides us with valuable information on the patterning of the limbs which helps to keep the nerve endings in the brain developing. If this were not happening, the baby could not learn.

As the baby grows into the child, we are faced with different considerations. For children the move from home to school is difficult and they can lose their natural grace and poise as they learn to fit in with their peer group and begin the slow process of acquiring new skills. One of the skills that causes great problems is writing. Children and students slump forward over the desk or table, their heads often resting on their arms and gripping the pen or pencil with great determination. Writing used to present fewer difficulties when a sloping surface instead of a flat one was used to support the paper. The hand was at a better angle for writing and the back could be kept more upright – just hold a book at an angle and see how much easier it is to read.

A lot of energy is wasted pushing the pen with accompanying frustration. Clear, legible writing can be produced but at the cost of considerable, unnecessary tension. If a little time were spent thinking how to sit and hold the pen before beginning to write, much heartache could be avoided. The guidelines on pages 50–53 give more detail on this procedure.

'Trying' to work

Easy does it!

We saw in Chapter 1 that many children hold their breath. This can come from a variety of sources – anger, frustration, concentration, waiting for their turn to perform an action – but the result is always the same. The functioning of the child becomes less efficient. Teaching our children to remember to breathe out is very important – then the breath can come in. This is called 'inspiration' and has a second meaning: that some divine influence, larger than the self, is lending a helping hand in the endeavour. Sometimes the bored child simply needs to get the respiratory system going so that he can think of something to do. Teaching children how to learn is fundamentally important before they can learn any new skill. 'There's nothing to do' might be eliminated if we could teach our children to understand and appreciate how much is going on inside them and how they can participate in this game of life.

> **66** *The world is so full of a number of things*
> *I'm sure we should all be as happy as kings.* **99**
> *R.L. Stevenson*

Pregnancy – Creating A New Life

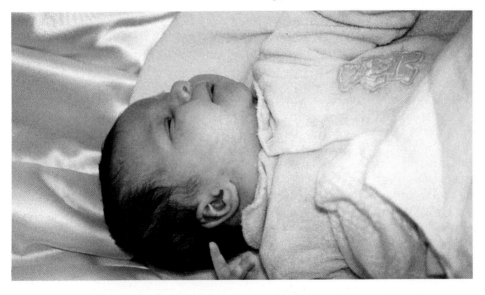

Pregnancy is a good time to consider your own body as well as the new body which you are creating inside yourself; this step into the unknown can give you the opportunity to change some of your old habits. In this time of enormous physical and psychological change, the Alexander Technique can be a constant and reassuring reference that you can take with you throughout pregnancy and into the actual birth.

So many changes are taking place in your body it is not surprising that you feel strange and may experience a great deal of discomfort, such as lower back pain. As your baby grows, the uterus gets bigger to accommodate the baby and you have more weight to carry in the front of your body. You have to think of balancing this extra weight and you counterbalance this forward pull by allowing your weight to go further back over your heels. During pregnancy it is very important to keep thinking of your back lengthening and widening and imagining your baby being connected to your spine. The back is there to act as a cradle for your baby; if he is comfortable and content, cradled inside you, there is a good chance that this contentment will continue when he is in his cradle in the outside world.

The widening of the back is important to prevent narrowing the space and restricting the baby. Think of your hip joints widening and opening and let your buttocks release down. We have already seen that fear tends to make us contract and this makes the space smaller and can squash your baby.

One of the popular recommendations during pregnancy at present is listening to music to soothe and calm you. You can do this when you take the weight off your feet in the Lying Down Procedure (see page 43). If you put your legs up on a chair, not only does it help to allow the pelvis to open and release, but it can also help to prevent *oedema*, the swelling of the ankles and legs. Lying down with your legs up is helpful for the first six months but after that it is better to lie on your side. Lying flat on your back can cause faintness due to the weight of the uterus pressing on two important veins which run along each side of the spine.

One of the most obvious changes in pregnancy is weight gain, around 26 lb in total. The Alexander Directions can help you keep in a balanced state as your weight increases and your centre of gravity alters.

The pumping power of the heart increases also and this can lead to upper chest breathing and breathlessness. The Direction to breathe out is very helpful here; practise the Whispered 'AH' (see page 58). Probably at no other time will you be so aware that 'Breath is life' as when you are breathing for two (or more).

During pregnancy your body produces a hormone called 'relaxin'. This secretion causes the ligaments to become softened and increases the flexibility of the joints in preparation for childbirth. Practise the Squat Procedure (see page 63) to keep the connections between ankles, knees, hips and back strong and free. You will also find this a useful position during labour.

Sometimes there is a problem with numbness in the hands and fingers. This is called the 'carpal tunnel syndrome' and can be helped considerably by practising the Crawling Procedure (see page 60). If you allow the weight to drop down through your wrists and hands it will help to relieve the build-up of pressure.

During the first stages of labour, it can be helpful to move about, thinking of your Directions and Walking Tall. The Alexander Technique will not take away the pain but you will have a better chance of dealing with it if you do not become tense and hold your breath. In between the contractions try some Whispered 'AH' sounds to keep your mind on breathing out and to help you relax.

Labour is a long journey, both for you and your baby, but keeping your principles of a free neck, stopping and saying 'No', and directing the whole body will help the process.

Caring For Your Baby

Once your baby has arrived, coping with all the new demands is very tiring. The old adage 'sleeping when the baby sleeps' is helpful, but if you cannot manage to sleep, try the Lying Down Procedure (see page 43) to give your body the time it needs to recover. Practising the Whispered 'AH' can help to restore a calm breathing pattern.

How you hold your baby is very important. If your hands are tense they can create a tense and tearful baby. We have all seen people who are good with dogs and horses; their very touch has an immediate soothing effect on the animals. Keeping your thoughts on your Directions for Use and thinking about not tightening your arms and wrists will make handling your baby easier and will help you to stay calmer.

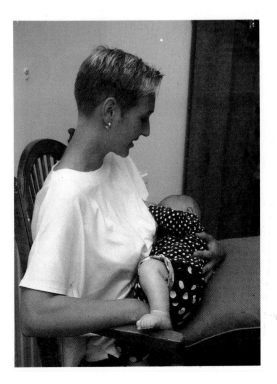

Holding your baby when feeding can cause tension in the neck and shoulder girdle, so try to check that you are sitting well, with good back support, and allow your shoulders to be wide and free. Try not to bend down in front as this can restrict your breathing. Put a pillow on your lap under the baby so that your baby's mouth is close to the breast or bottle. If you have an armchair, rest your arms on the arms of the chair.

In the night when the baby wakes, think of saying 'No' before you reach for him. Remember, if you arrive flustered, your baby will react to this and become upset. You are your child's first experience of how to deal with life, and he or she will imitate anything you do; when you smile he or she will smile, when you frown he or she will often burst out crying.

Babies' spines are very pliable, so remember to support their heads and backs whenever you pick them up and hold them.

When buying equipment for the baby look carefully at how it is designed. Some car seats and buggies give little support and the baby ends up collapsed down in front in a crumpled heap.

As babies grow into toddlers and become mobile and heavier, throughout the day you are running after them and picking them up. Often you have the youngster, the toys, the lunch and nappies to juggle with simultaneously. The Directions in the section on bending and lifting on page 65 will help you here.

The early years go by so quickly and in this time many things have to be learnt. You, as a parent, can demonstrate ease and grace and help prevent tension and anxiety in your children right from the start.

Children can be a handful, but they need not pull you down

Just as your children learn from you, you can learn to share their spontaneous joy of childhood and release into laughter

Education – Stop, Look and Listen

Learning at home

Children are by nature inquisitive. As they grow up and begin to experience the world, each day brings new and exciting discoveries and their enthusiasm is boundless. They love to take things apart to see how they work. 'Why?' is one of their favourite words. They want to know what is in any parcel and what is behind every locked door. If you say something is dangerous they must do it. As parents, we are faced with the dilemma, 'How do I keep this spirit of exploration alive and yet prepare my child for the trials of life?'.

When you are bringing up very small children there is a wonderful question you can ask them. It is, 'Do you know the magic word?' 'No', says the child. 'That's it – No *is* the magic word'. 'No' can be as positive as it can be negative. The way we teach inhibition (the way to stop) is very important. The introduction to 'No' as a positive, magic word, is essential. We have to remember that children need to be encouraged to stop and be given the time and confidence to make choices for themselves.

In early growth and development children always take their time. We, as parents, interfere with this and cause problems by urging them to hurry up – 'Come on, we haven't got all day!'. We get into the habit of trying to fit so much into each day that the strain soon begins to tell on our children. The time we used to have to simply 'stop and stare' seems to have vanished. When did we last watch some simple event in nature, such as ants carrying a leaf or a bird building a nest?

Children too get caught in the trap of going too fast and not really looking at things. This also applies to listening. Often we hear the complaint that the child has switched off and does not hear what we are saying. Sometimes we blame this on the sheer level of noise that surrounds us in our urban lifestyle – radios, walkmen plugged in the ears, piped music in many public places and even a little tune on the phone while we are waiting for our call to be connected all fill the air with sound-waves. We develop the habit of blocking out these background sounds and get used to not really listening.

We become used to not stopping, not looking and not listening, and after a while this begins to feel normal and right to us. As Alexander stressed, 'The stupidity of letting children go wrong is that once they go wrong their right is wrong: therefore the more they try to be right, the more they go wrong.'

By encouraging our children to become more aware of their bodies and how they use them and teaching them the magic word 'No', we will be giving them a good start. They will be able to achieve the skill which the eminent educationalist, Professor John Dewey, described as 'Thinking in activity' and this will prepare them for the rigours of school.

Learning at School

When children begin school, they are given a barrage of instructions. Most of these are to do with getting it right. They are told to 'Sit up straight', 'Speak up', 'Take a deep breath', 'See how quietly you can walk', 'See how quick you can be'. Suddenly they are being told to do many new things in a precise way. Children can feel threatened by all these demands and their attempts to carry out instructions are often doomed.

They want so much to do well but trying to be right often ends up in comparative failure. Their success or failure is measured by the Testing System, either the weekly variety or the Public Examination. Frightened of making mistakes, the child begins to hold the breath, stiffen and tense the whole body. Some children can become so tense that they literally shake. In this state, the child's young and underdeveloped mental apparatus is put on the rack, and yet often his intellectual status and educational fate depend on these tests. The results of the tests are meant to give a reliable guide to children's future careers but when children are frightened, they cannot show their natural ability. The 'startle pattern reflex', referred to on page 27, occurs, and this stressful reaction leads to a disapointing end result. Moreover, the more often a child is unsuccessful, the more likely he is to give up and not try at all. So from being stiff, nervous wrecks, children can become unmotivated lumps, slumping all day at desks, and sprawling all night in front of the television. The recent increase in childhood obesity and heart attacks bears sad evidence to this new 'couch potato' attitude.

However, in many schools the pendulum has swung the other way; rigorous testing has been thrown out and freedom of expression has been adopted as the basis for education. This freedom does not include the important ability of being able to stop. Often what is meant by 'freedom' is that the people in authority have lost interest and cannot impose discipline. The children sense that the boat has no rudder and become anxious from lack of leadership. The Alexander Technique with its joint threads of stopping (inhibition) and leading (direction) is a good basis on which to begin any form of education. The Latin phrase *mens sana in sano corpore* – 'a sound mind in a sound body' has been used for centuries as the stated educational goal of many schools. The Alexander Technique can help this goal become a reality.

Growing old gracefully

As we get older, we can become worried that we are going to be a burden, not only to ourselves but to our families and friends. Records show that people are living longer today; life expectancy is now about 75 across Europe compared with 47 in Britain at the beginning of the century. Medical science has made extraordinary breakthroughs in treating successfully many of the once fatal diseases and surgery can replace some parts worn out by wear and tear. The number of years we have is greater, but what about the quality of life? As we age, we begin to notice little things starting to go wrong. We lose some of our energy and things seem to take more time to do. We find the print in the telephone directory is too small and the step up on to the bus is too big. Things begin to trouble us; we are unsure about the future. Sometimes this anxiety leads to breathlessness and even pain in our chests.

A contributing factor to these problems is that we have become less mobile. We are designed for movement and expect to be able to do what we wish to. If over the years we have been putting our bodies through the obstacle course of life with ever more determination to push on, then it is time to stop and reconsider how we are treating our body. It has served us well, but it needs a chance to recover and reorganise itself for the second half of our life.

Sometimes people think they are too old to change the habits of a lifetime. As long as you can think and you wish to change, then it is possible. People cannot be assessed simply in years. Your biological age (the state of your mind and body) is often not the same as your chronological age (the actual number of years you have lived). We have all heard of people whose doctors have told them that their heart and lungs are those of a person half their age.

F.M. Alexander lived to be 86 and was teaching the week before he died. Perhaps we have misunderstood the ageing process. We know that brain cells are dying off at an alarming rate, so we expect memory lapses and corresponding inefficiency. But while the brain cells are dying, the nerve endings of the brain can continue to grow, provided they are stimulated. So an important duty for us is to keep the nerves stimulated. This can be done in a variety of ways, but one reliable source of stimulation for the mind is the body. The mind and body are on a loop system, so we can get changes in brain patterning by changing body patterning. The work done at the Institute for Human Potential found many interesting facts about continuing growth in the area of nerve endings and it showed how stimulation improved cognitive and learning skills.

When you practise the Alexander Technique with its Instructions for Use, Stopping and Directions, you can give your body and your mind a chance to function efficiently and to continue learning. Alexander liked to refer to himself as a 'learner', rather than a teacher. The memory and patterns of the past are important, but they need not be like old suitcases that are weighing you down. Alexander said, 'We can throw away the habit of a lifetime in a few minutes if we use our brain'.

Each day could be a new beginning, a chance to experiment on yourself. In this interesting time of your life, all your past experience could contribute positively to a new way of being. The Alexander Technique does not promise miracle rejuvenation but it could help you to stop getting short of breath and keep a spring in your step. All the procedures are safe, because you go at your own pace and because they are about 'how *not* to' – how not to hold your breath, how not to slump, how not to stiffen and how not to worry. There is nothing too fast about the Alexander Technique; it is more like travelling in a carriage than in Concorde.

3

PRACTICAL PROCEDURES

How to lie down

Every time we say, 'Take the weight off your feet', or 'Just lie down for a while and you'll feel better', or 'I am longing to lie down', or 'I can't hold myself up any longer', we are stating a very important fact: our bodies need to lie down. Gravity is constantly exerting pressure on us in the upright position. So when we lie down, the floor is supporting us and the body has a chance to stop holding itself up and release and open out. Gravity is still operating but in a different way, so that the pressure exerted creates the chance for more space and release (particularly in the ribcage) to happen.

At the end of the day we rest. If we can get a good night's sleep we feel set up for the next day but if we are agitated and sleepless, that distress continues through the day. The general pattern is to be active for about 12 hours and to rest or sleep for about eight hours. To deprive someone of sleep amounts to torture. Growth in children is restricted if they do not get enough rest.

When we lie down changes take place in the body which are beneficial to our general health. Do not feel that it is a bad thing to take time to lie down in the day. Here is how to set yourself up to get the most out of the time you spend lying down.

Find a quiet place at home or work with a dry, warm floor. You will need to put something underneath your head to give it a little support. If you lie flat on the floor, the head tends to fall back and the lower back leaves the floor.

You may use a book or a telephone directory or even your briefcase if it is a flat one. The optimum height underneath the head varies from person to person, but about 2–3 inches is a starting point. You should not feel restricted in the throat; that could mean that the support is a little bit too high. If you find your head falling back and the lower back arching, you probably need more height under the head. Usually it is better for the support under the head to be too high than too low.

So now you have chosen your head support, place it on the floor and sit on the floor in front of it ready to lean back and lie down.

Do not just collapse backwards with no thought as to 'how' you are lying. Stop and remember about your back lengthening and widening before you unfold yourself on to the floor, dropping back carefully.

Now you are lying flat on your back with your head supported by the book underneath your head. Your legs are flat on the floor in front of you. Bring them up one at a time so they are bent with the heels fairly near your body.

Now you have your back flat on the floor, not by pushing down but by just allowing the weight to drop. This may take more time than you think, but be patient. The head is supported and the legs are bent. Fold the arms over the body so the hands are resting on the lower ribcage and you can feel the movement of the ribs as the air comes in and out.

It is important to have both ends of the body (the head and the feet) positioned in this way so that the whole torso is resting on the flat surface. This position is called the 'semi-supine' (half lying down).

Now you are ready to begin *thinking*. Lying down is such a restful activity that we tend to close our eyes and possibly doze off. So keep your

eyes open and make use of your constructive rest time to change many of
the bad physical habits that you have adopted over the years. The
number of years does not matter. Even little children benefit enormously
by giving their bodies this time to recover from the stresses and strains of
the day.

Now to get on with the thinking. Thinking is going on all the time in
our brains. In order to think we need oxygen, so breathe out, then shut
your mouth; the air will come in through your nose and fill up your
lungs. Your hands are on your lower ribs, just above your waist, and you
can experience the movements of your ribs moving in and out. The air
should be coming in low down, not only in the upper chest.

We saw in the X-ray of the chest on page 13 how the space changes in the lungs. As you get this breathing pattern going, you may begin to feel calmer. In this quiet state you may notice that as you stop holding on, letting the ribs widen, the back begins to lengthen. The weight of the body drops down and your breathing gets easier and deeper. There may still be areas of tightness in your body, places where you are holding on. Do not try to do anything about this by pushing or stretching, just wait.

Unlike the upright position, you do not have the problem of balancing your heavy head, so the muscles at the back of the neck have a chance to release. By taking the pressure off the spine, it can lengthen and become springy. Remember, your spine is made up of discs and bones. The discs are like cushions that can get squashed when you are standing up. In the lying down position they plump up again, the spine becomes less like a stiff rod and gravity takes the strain off the ribs and allows them to spring apart more easily.

- Think of the weight dropping down through the back of the head.

- Think of the weight dropping down through the shoulders.

- Think of the weight dropping down through the hips.

- Now think of the weight dropping down through the feet.

Letting the weight drop down is very useful for releasing the muscles in the front of the body – often we have been tightening too much in front. Make sure that you are not pushing or holding the breath. Practise the semi-supine position for about 15–20 minutes every day.

When you decide to get up, it is important *how* you do this. You do not want to lose the benefit that you have gained. Stretch one arm upwards, with your hand pointing up to the ceiling, then let the hand point across

your body and roll over on to your side. Now bring your hands and knees underneath your body, so you are on all fours, like a baby in the crawling position, with weight placed evenly under the shoulders and hips.

Slowly rock forwards and backwards gathering momentum until you come back to sitting on your heels. Gradually come up until you are on your knees then, letting the head lead you, stand up. You will notice that you feel taller, lighter and often clearer in your thoughts. Sometimes people describe this feeling as being more 'awake'. To be more awake is to be more aware of yourself and what is going on around you. It is a good state to be in, as you can operate more efficiently.

Sitting

We spend a good deal of time sitting in chairs. Very often we are not comfortable. We are putting strain on our back and considerable pressure on the abdomen (this has been calculated as about 18 lb of pressure if we are sitting slumped). When we slump forward we restrict our breathing. We can also slump backwards, sitting on our tailbones and causing great pressure on the lower spine.

Watching small children, we notice they often squat instead of sit. Squatting is better for the back and the vital organs than sitting but as we grow up convention dictates that the chair is more appropriate than the floor, so we sit. We have periods of enforced sitting when we are driving in cars or travelling in planes. When we get up from these seats we are often very stiff and it takes some time to get moving again.

Guidelines to follow
Before you sit, take a little time to think about your total length from your head to your feet before you bend your knees. There is always time for this quick thought even if you are longing to flop into the chair. *How*

you sit down makes a big difference to the activity of sitting. Sitting is not passive; you need to be conscious of yourself in the chair. Remember the three joints that make this movement possible: the pivot joint which allows the head to nod gently forwards on the neck, the ball and socket joints, which allow the hips to move backwards, and the hinge joints, which allow the knees to bend. So let the head go forwards and your knees bend and the hips go backwards – like an anglepoise lamp. Think of the back lengthening and widening until the seat of the chair interrupts this partial squat. Then let the back straighten up.

Check that you are not perching (i.e. sitting precariously on the edge) in the chair. Think of the weight going down through the sitting bones till you are sitting upright in the chair. Sometimes we have learnt an unnatural way of sitting by being told as children to 'Sit up straight'. If we contract and try to pull ourselves up we risk restricting the breathing by holding the breath as we narrow our bodies and keep the spine inflexible.

You can check how you move from standing to sitting and begin to be aware of maintaining the length of the body before you sit and when you are sitting. Sitting can be easy and balanced if you stop collapsing into the chair or sitting like a ramrod.

Applied sitting

Writing at a desk and working at a computer

When your chair is in front of your computer, table or desk you immediately have the stimulus to pull down in front as you get on with your typing or writing. Very often you are so concerned with the end result you give no thought to how you work.

Here are some guidelines to help you when sitting and working with your eyes and hands.

Make sure your chair is at a good height to reach the surface in front of you. As you sit, lift the arms and place the backs of your hands on the surface of the desk and try not to lift your shoulders as you do this.

Breathe out and then turn your hands over so that they are flat on the surface with your fingers lengthening out. Your arms should be bent at about 90° (right angles) and if this is not so, then perhaps the chair is too low or too high. Do not adapt yourself to the equipment; change the chair rather than squash your spine. Adjust the furniture to accommodate you.

Think of your shoulders, elbows and wrists as connecting tunnels. If you think of them as joints you tend to stiffen and contract them, rather than release and create space in them. Remember that they are joined to your back like wings and when the breath comes in, the upper neck widens between your shoulder wings. Think of plenty of space being available under your armpits. When you bend forward towards the desk, do not slump forward, but bend like an anglepoise lamp from the hips. This will help you to stop crumpling the front of your body and squashing the ribs. If you pull down in front, you will limit the amount of air in the lungs and then you will start gasping the air in, upsetting the respiratory pattern. When you have no air, no breath, no energy, you push yourself more and more and achieve less and less.

If you are working at a keyboard, check the appropriate levels of the desk and chair, take your hands off the table and allow the arms to drop down to the sides, like wings in the resting position, with the fingers pointing freely to the floor. Now place your hands on the keyboard and begin the free movement of your fingers. Try to take short breaks to keep the arms, wrists and fingers supple.

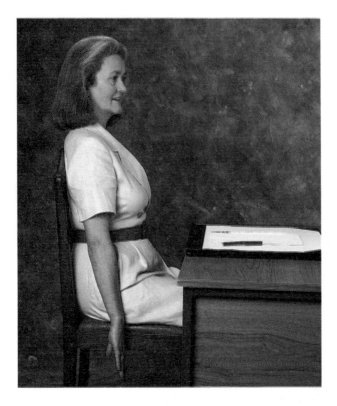

When you come to write, one of the first requirements is that the surface you use is sloped. This is not difficult, as a piece of board, a tray or a large book can be used by putting a support behind it to make a sloping surface. This creates far less strain on the wrists and eyes.

Place your hand palm down on the table, then flex the wrist backwards. This little movement is very helpful in stopping the tendency to pick up a pen or pencil by grasping it and then holding it too tightly. It allows for space in the wrist (carpal tunnel) and the stretch which is created in the wrist helps with the problem of repetitive strain injury, in which space becomes limited and release difficult and subsequent pain results, often leading to loss of use of the fingers.

Place the first finger and thumb together and gently flex them. Then, pick up the pen and hold it lightly between the fingers and thumb. Try not to grab the pen or to grasp it too tightly and do not put too much effort into this small action. Flex the fingers again while holding the pen. Now place the tip of the pen on the paper and begin to make some marks.

The use of our hands has enabled us to evolve. Being able to write has allowed humanity to develop and communicate and this precious skill need not cause us trouble and pain.

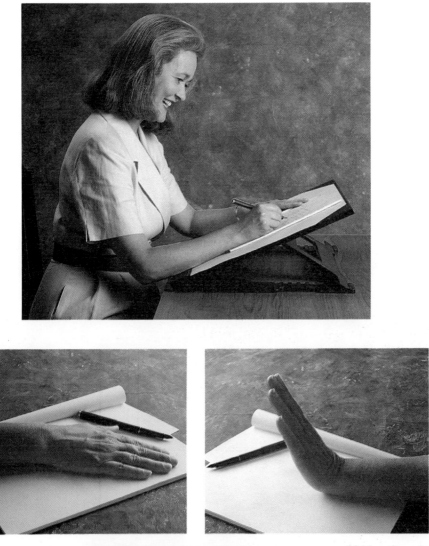

Flexing the wrist

Holding the pen

Playing the piano

Keyboard musicians find that taking a little bit of time before playing helps to prevent the pain in the neck, upper back and wrists which so often accompanies performance.

Follow the same procedures as for desk work. Because the keyboard of the piano is flat, it is very important to keep thinking of the head going forward and up and the back lengthening and the shoulder blades going back and down, so that the arms can remain free. When the elbows are bent, think of the weight dropping down from the shoulders through the elbows. Think of lengthening along the forearm right to the fingertips, and remember to keep breathing. When a musical passage is fast or difficult, try not to hold the breath or raise the shoulders.

Nelly Ben-Or, a concert pianist and Alexander Teacher has found that often 'the player works harder to "get" more out of the instrument by using sheer force. Thus he increases his misuse by creating growing tensions and interference with what Alexander called the Primary Control. The more misuse sets in, the harder the player feels he has to work. The harder he works, the more physical tension he uses; the more he gets locked into an experience of struggling with the resistance of the keys and so becomes convinced that he must develop strength of fingers. Thus a vicious circle of growing misuse and difficulties becomes established.'

Walk tall

When we walked on all four legs the head led and the body followed in the same horizontal plane. The direction of the head and the direction in which the body went were the same. The eyes saw something, possibly food, and the body quite literally 'headed' for it.

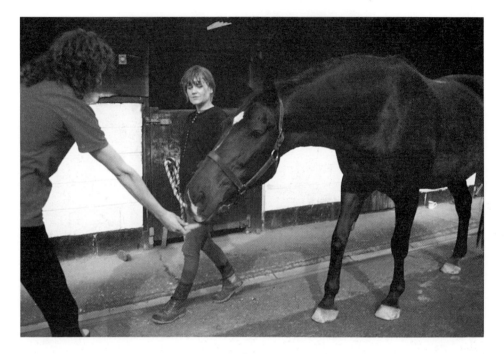

In four-legged animals the direction of the head is the same as the direction of movement – both are forward

When we stood up movement became more complicated. We no longer have the stability of a leg at each corner of our body. We are balanced almost on tiptoes, with a heavy head poised in space on top of a waving spine. Professor Dart has called us the 'tottering biped' – we are in a state of unstable equilibrium. The direction of the head and body are no longer the same. The spine is going up to the head in a vertical direction but we move forward in a horizontal direction. If we are not careful we will end up moving forward by dropping our heads down and leaning forward too much. Over the years this can cause us to become bent over. Sometimes this bad posture is a result of illness or injury but often it is our haste to move forward which has distorted us.

Guidelines to follow

In order to go forward, it is helpful in the first instance to take a step backwards. There are two reasons for this. Firstly, we do not normally walk backwards, so it breaks the prescribed patterns for walking which we may have. Secondly, the step back gives a chance for the weight to go back over the heels so the balance is different. Too often we are falling forward when we walk. We want to stay back from the objective and achieve a gliding movement instead of a snatch and grab action.

So the important points to remember are:

* Stand tall – just by thinking about lengthening, not pushing.

* Stand equally on your feet. The weight should be distributed between three points:

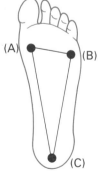

Weight distribution through the foot

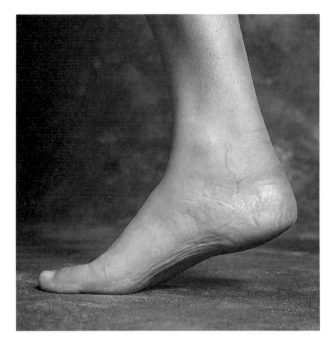

The spring reflex

The arch of the foot should be lively, like a bubbling spring. Flat feet have no arch and no spring.

When you decide to move your foot, just let the heel come off the ground, then lift the foot and place it behind you. Keep the movement light and effortless. If you have the benefit of a teacher, he or she will help you in this by giving support to the body, so you can let the leg move very freely. Having practised the step backwards, you can now try the more conventional way of walking. I am not suggesting you should take a backward step every time, but it is a good way of checking that you are keeping your knees and ankles as free as possible.

As you keep thinking of your Directions, allow the heel to leave the floor, let the foot go forward and touch the ground, then transfer the weight on to this foot. All the time, the spine is at full stretch with the head going forward and up and the back is lengthening and widening. So you have moved forward and the second leg is ready to lift off from the heel and travel forward, left, right, left, right, left, right, a cross pattern reflex of progressive forward movement.

Be careful that you do not fall forward – imagine the wind is behind you and you can let that force from behind take you forward. If you begin to notice that you have lost the length and stretch in your spine, then maybe you are trying too hard or going too fast. Walking is excellent exercise, but the benefit is lost if you contract and push rather than lengthening and gliding.

The whispered 'AH' – how to produce sound without effort

The sound 'AH', as in 'father', is a long vowel sound which keeps the air passage open and clear. When you whisper, you can hear if something in the voice is not working properly. The aim of the whispered 'AH' is to practise using an unrestricted flow of air in a non-habitual way. You are learning to make a sound without any effort.

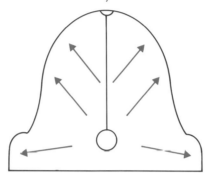

All sound is made up of vibrations. A bell rings because there is space inside it, space for the vibrations to work. If the vibrations are working then there will be resonance. When you hear a voice which sounds large and full you can be sure that the voice has enough space in which to work. The reverse is true when you are frightened or angry; your voice becomes small and cramped, or even disappears completely.

It is natural to have a big, free voice. Every baby knows about this; sometimes it is impossible to believe the volume of noise coming out of such a small person for such a long time. It is useful to practise the whispered 'AH' in order to regain the full size and freedom of your voice.

Guidelines to follow

Stand in front of the mirror and gently blow the air out through your mouth. Watch your upper chest and shoulders and check that they do not move too much. There will be a little movement, but your chest should remain fairly balanced and stable. Allow your head to nod gently forward. At the end of each breath, shut your mouth and notice how the air comes back in through the nostrils. Do not sniff the air in, as this will narrow the nasal passages and restrict the amount which gets into the lungs. Sniffing may mean you are taking your breath in forcibly, rather than trusting that it will come in naturally.

After about five or six outbreaths, look at yourself and think of something funny which makes you smile. The smile begins in your eyes, which light up, and then you cannot help the mouth smiling and your facial muscles softening. On the inside, more space is created at the back of the mouth as the soft palate lifts. You have found extra space with no extra effort.

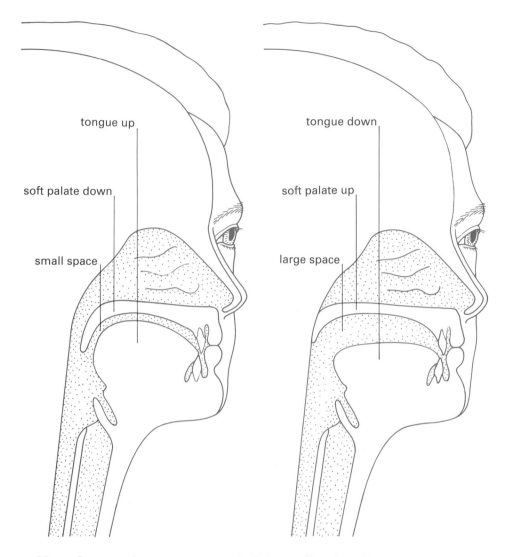

tongue up

tongue down

soft palate down

soft palate up

small space

large space

Now observe what your tongue is doing. Allow it to lie on the floor of your mouth, with the tip against the lower teeth. Again, this is to create as much space and freedom as possible. Your tongue can be tight and bunched up, reducing the space in your mouth. This can lead to you being tongue tied and cause difficulty in making enough sound to be heard. The harder you try to speak up, the tighter and weaker your voice becomes. Remember that in order to make any sound there has to be enough space and a free air flow.

So now you are ready to make a sound, the sound 'AH', in a whisper. Just let the jaw fall open and whisper 'AH', a soft, open, easy sound. You are conscious of how you are making it, but not putting undue effort into it. When you get to the end of the breath, shut your mouth and the air will come in through your nose. As soon as that happens, whisper another 'AH'.

- Think of something funny that makes you smile.
- Put your tongue to the back of your lower teeth.
- Let your jaw fall open and say 'AH' in a whispered tone.
- Shut your mouth and allow the air in.

Repeat the procedure about 5–6 times. You are learning consciously to think about the outbreath, so that the inbreath, or inspiration, may take place.

> **66** *Inspiration cannot be bought or forced; it is a gift freely given.* **99**

Practising this each day will lead to more awareness of what you are doing when you make sounds. It also has the benefit of regulating your breathing so that you will be calm before speaking rather than uptight. Rather than rushing to answer the telephone as soon as it rings, try to do a whispered 'AH' before you pick up the receiver to speak. It can make a big difference to how you sound.

Crawling – moving on all fours

Why should crawling help you change and become more consciously aware of yourself? We are at the end of a long line of vertebrate development. When we stood up on our back legs, we took a big decision which made us physically unstable and vulnerable, with our soft underbellies exposed.

Babies have to learn how to stand on their own two feet. They begin by inching along on their stomachs, then getting up on their hands and knees and then moving forward on all fours. Anyone who has children knows that the sudden extension of frontiers which crawling provides means that nothing is safe. In fact, if a baby does not crawl, reading difficulties can result from missing out on this vital stage of development.

Doctors Dolman and Delcato have done extensive research on the importance of crawling, the cross pattern reflex, in the development and growth of the nerve endings in the brain. So do not think you are regressing by crawling; you are enabling neurological development to continue and by returning to all fours, you get a clearer idea of the relationship of the back to the limbs. The back muscles have a chance to lengthen and widen while following the lead of the head. Some people find that crawling helps them if they have to learn speeches, lines or songs by heart.

Guidelines to follow

Carefully lower yourself on to your knees one at a time. Bend forward and place your hands on the floor in front of you. Check that each hand is directly underneath the corresponding shoulder and that each knee is directly underneath the corresponding hip. You need to be evenly balanced, like a four-legged animal. Begin to rock gently backwards and forwards on your hands and knees.

Now turn your head to the side and look at your right hand. As you do this you will notice that you turn slightly towards that side. Now let the left knee and the right hand move forward together. Make the movement fairly small and do not overstretch yourself. Watch as you make this movement that you do not hollow the back. If you let your head lead your body, your back will remain flat and stretched.

So you have moved forward with your opposite hand and foot. You have engaged the cross pattern reflex and let the spiral action of the torso happen. Turn your head back to the centre and repeat the procedure. Look to the left hand and move the right knee and left hand forward at the same time. Do not lift the knee and hand from the floor, just slide forward, letting the head lead the body. Check that your feet are just dragging along behind you and that your toes are not curled under. Then look back to centre and repeat the procedure, right and left together, left and right together. You will gain a momentum and a rhythm. When you get familiar with crawling forwards, try doing it backwards.

The cross pattern reflex

Crawling can help with the problem of stiff wrists. The weight of the body going down through the arm and then the wrist without stress seems to give the tunnels of the wrist a chance to open up. It is as if you are using your hands as feet, so instead of contracting the muscles and grasping and holding you are extending the muscles into a weight-bearing activity. This reverses the way you normally use your hands and can help with repetitive strain injuries, which are often caused by using the hands and arms in the same contracted position for too long.

Try to do some crawling every day, and if you have a baby, check that he or she is getting a daily dose of this excellent co-ordinating exercise. It is also a very beneficial procedure when you are pregnant.

As the uterus gets larger, the extra weight can pull you forward and down and narrow the back, causing lower back pain. When you adopt the crawling position you create a secure base on all fours. The spine acts as the girder from which the baby is slung and the pull forward, which happens when standing, is prevented. Automatically, the back lengthens and widens, which can help relieve the pain. This position can be used when the actual birth is taking place.

Squatting – sitting without a chair

The chair is a relatively modern invention and before it existed we either sat on the ground or we squatted. Small children still squat as their basic way of lowering themselves to perform any activity.

Squatting has a very positive effect on the whole body, especially the back, legs and vital organs. It is good and healthy to be able to squat but for many of us, as we stiffen up, it can be difficult at first. When you try this procedure, use a little support in the form of holding on the banisters or a heavy table, or even a friend's helping hands. Make sure that who or what you hold on to is strong enough to take your weight.

Guidelines to follow

Stand with your head going forward and up, your back long and wide and your feet apart. Each foot should be directly under the corresponding hip, but wide enough apart to let the body move between the legs. Let the head pivot forward on the neck and keeping your heels flat on the floor, bend the ankles and the knees and let the hips move backwards. Try not to curve the spine, but keep the back long and stretched. At first, your heels may tend to come off the floor, but with time and perseverance you will be able to get down to the floor with the feet still flat.

*Peter Fisher of the
National Back Pain
Committee working with
a patient*

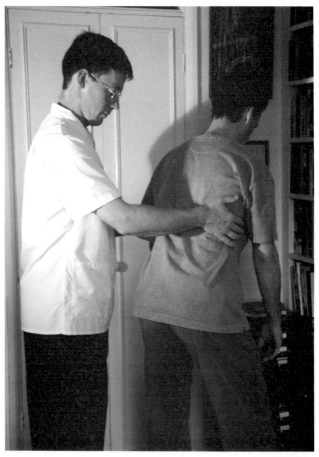

The ability to adopt this squatting posture in comfortable equilibrium is a prerequisite to the poised upright posture. In the long course of evolution, the squat was an important stage in the development of the human skill of standing completely upright on two feet.

As your head flies forward, let your hips go backwards and your knees and ankles bend, until you end up as low as you can go. Some people get down straight away, but for others it may be more difficult because of stiffness in the joints and muscles or the unfamiliarity of the movement. If you take time to practise the squat, you will gain more mobility and put less strain on your back and legs when you have to lift something. Peter Fisher, the Alexander Teacher on the Educational Board of the National Back Pain Association, says, 'Learning to squat is very important when we are dealing with back pain. It is a simple but effective way to improve the strength and mobility of the back.'

Bending and lifting – standing up and bending down

We bend because we need to be lower than when we are standing up. We need to pick up the shopping, tie our shoe-laces, weed the garden, lift up the children, trim the edge of the lawn or make the bed. All these actions require some degree of supple movement and freedom in our joints.

As we get older, stiffness and pain can result from bending in the wrong way. We tend to expect bending to cause us pain and sometimes decide to do it as little as possible. This leads to more stiffness in our joints and even less ability to bend and the vicious circle continues.

We can break this pattern by learning how to bend so that the appropriate muscles can do their work. We have it in our minds that bending means bending down and this is where part of the problem lies. As we go down, we contract and shorten ourselves instead of keeping a good stretch in our back muscles and freedom and length in our leg muscles. Small children move up and down with great freedom and suppleness and they manage to bend and lift things without stress and effort. We have got into bad habits which make us too stiff and rigid when we try to lower ourselves.

The problem is made even worse when we try to lift something. Then the weight of the object is added to the weight that gravity is exerting on us, great strain is put on our backs and legs and we become increasingly weak and feeble. It should be possible to bend without causing undue pressure on ourselves.

Guidelines to follow

Place your feet securely apart with the weight evenly distributed. The lower you need to bend, the further apart your feet will have to be. Bend your ankles and your knees and let your head go forward and your hips bend. You may find that you begin to tighten in the legs, especially the thighs, so think of lengthening along the back a little bit more and let the weight go down through your heels.

The thigh muscles are very strong and often do more than their share of the work. It is the long back muscles which should be stretching and releasing in this position. The back muscles need to be strong and the back ribs should be wide and moving freely with each breath. The thighs should give support without stiffening and the ankles and knees should be freely released.

Bending should be an action which keeps you moving and does not get you into a fixed position. If you continued bending down, you would end up squatting. Think of the guidelines:

- Let your neck be free.

- Let your head go forward and up.

- Let your back lengthen and widen.

Then you are ready to bend:

- Let your head move forward.

- Let your knees bend.

- Let your hips move backwards.

Bending in this way can help keep the joints supple. Remember not to hold your breath or to try too hard. Try not to slump forward and arch the back, but keep all the muscles lengthened and the joints released.

When you come to lift something, remember to counterbalance the weight of the object by allowing your own body weight to go back and down through your heels.

4

PRACTICAL APPLICATIONS

Acting

ROBERT MACDONALD Alexander Teacher, London Academy of
Music and Dramatic Art

The actor recreates human experience. His art is to fill every moment of his stage activity, from the commonplace to the extraordinary and the unexpected, with understanding, sympathy and insight. The actor draws on his own experiences of life. His attention to people and the world around him gives him the necessary experience to draw on and create from. Often in our haste we block the senses and miss out on the richness and complexity of life. By applying the Alexander Technique, we free the senses and we begin to look and listen to our full capacity. As we become more conscious of how we interact with the world, we realise that our often habitual mental patterns block the sympathetic response and broader vision that is fundamental to the actor's craft.

Acting requires a balance of energy in the performer: calm and still, yet full of energy and ready to act; a strong sense of self, while maintaining an expanded awareness and an openness to listen and to be moved by the other actors; to be clear and definite in action, yet to move in such a way that the imagination and intuition are awakened; to explore the rational and the emotional so that neither compromises the other. The Alexander Technique helps the actor to realise that there is no separation between these different facets of his performance. It helps him to experience all his faculties and resources working as a unified response to a situation.

An increase of energy prior to performance is a necessary and natural preparation, but if this over-excites our fear of failure then it can be a strong stimulus to stiffen the neck, hold the breath and to try too hard. As a result all the audience sees is an actor struggling with his personal habits and mannerisms, leading to characterisation that is one-sided and predictable. The Alexander Technique explores an effortless, energised starting point and a way of working that leads to freedom in activity, an understanding of the process of inspiration, and an openness that allows a performance to be enlivened by and resonate the deeper levels of human experience.

> 66 *What a piece of work is a man, how noble in reason, how infinite in faculties, in form and moving how express and admirable, in action how like an angel, in apprehension how like a god; the beauty of the world, the paragon of animals.* 99
>
> *William Shakespeare*

Bicycling

BARRY COLLINS   Alexander Teacher and Dental Surgeon

It's not really surprising that cyclists do sometimes experience back pain –
just look around at passing cyclists and see how many of them collapse
forward from the highly damageable lumbar region of their lower backs
and how few have any awareness of maintaining the natural curve in that
area.

If you lose the integrity of the back, you have lost the anchor point and
the beam from which the muscle attachments for legs and arms originate.
Collapsing the back produces, in turn, a collapse in the front, which
restricts rib movement and breathing.

You get the most oxygen for the least effort from the floating ribs at
the bottom of the ribcage. These lower ribs hinge to the spine at the back
but are free at their front end. They are very much more mobile than
their neighbours which are fixed at both ends. Collapsing forward
restricts their freedom and much more effort is needed to use
inappropriate upper ribs and accessory breathing muscles.

The accessory muscles are those that try to raise and expand the top of
the ribcage, the very inflexible part, and should only be involved during
maximum effort. But in the average individual, demonstrating what
Alexander would call 'poor use', it is these accessory muscles which have
become the primary breathing muscles, at the expense of the under-used
and far more effective lower ribs.

So neck muscles must be as released as possible, otherwise (if nothing
else) the effect is like wearing a crash helmet with the straps permanently
over-tightened and is, in a word, *painful*.

Perhaps you can now begin to understand that cycling efficiently and
effectively is a process of recognising and then stripping away
inappropriate muscle effort that is being generated at your own physical
expense but which adds not one iota to the forward movement of the
bike.

Dancing

MADELEINE WHITE   Ex-soloist Sadlers Wells Royal Ballet, Classical Ballet Teacher

As an ex-professional dancer myself and a teacher of ballet for 20 years, I have found that once they start, dancers respond well to the Alexander Technique. They find that breathing is freer and the body responds more willingly to the unnatural demands put on it – turning the leg out to achieve a fine pointed foot and beauty of line can be crippling in later life.

A number of classical dancers have benefited from the Alexander Technique – usually after taking Alexander lessons when recuperating from illness or injury. They have nothing but praise for the way they have been taught to use thought in movement, to conserve energy and to release and lengthen the spine so that it can have the freedom and 'spring' with which to absorb the impact of landing from a jump.

The ballet class always starts with work at the barre. If students hang on to the barre like parrots on a perch they are going to distort their balance mechanism by tightening from their hand through to the arm, the shoulder and the neck. They have to learn to find the true centre of gravity of their bodies while practising the demanding stretches which they need to do. When they leave the practice barre and start performing on the stage this balance becomes even more important.

Dancers often suffer from depression. This could be attributed to the common fault of breathing with the midriff muscles held in. The balance of oxygen and carbon dioxide in the blood is disturbed by upper chest breathing, leading to feelings of anxiety which causes depression.

Working with other dancers, in *pas de deux*, for example, needs rapport between partners. They can feel the balance and flow of movement between and through each other so much better if they are not holding their breath and over-tensing. The Alexander Technique teaches them to keep their muscles toned so that they use the correct balance of contraction and release for particular movements. There is more time than they think to perform a movement – to hear the melody and rhythms of the music, to express emotions, and even more importantly, to *enjoy* dancing.

Driving

CHRISTOPHER BATTEN   Alexander Teacher and Marketing Consultant

Driving can be hell! Just sit in a car and it's uphill – the seat slopes, your hips tilt backwards and your lower back sags. If your spine doesn't tell you that this is wrong at the time, it certainly will later. Driving is one of the major causes of lower back pain.

Then there's the stress. The mildest characters become demons, other drivers the enemy, and the roads, the traffic – well, they're the pits. But with Alexander you can turn this round. Driving is a skilled activity largely under habitual control, so it's an excellent area in which to apply the Technique. What's more, when you're doing this, you don't have the feeling that it's interrupting or slowing down what you're meant to be doing.

When you get into the driving seat, pause and check yourself out. Lift your bottom off the seat and tuck it right back into the corner. Let your back feel the support of the seat, especially across the width of the shoulders. Free the neck. Allow yourself to lengthen right up the back. And now breathe gently out.

Next check your mirror. Ten to one you'll see you need to adjust it upwards, because your back has lengthened and you're sitting higher and more alert.

As you drive off, notice your hands on the wheel. Are they clutching it tight? What about your elbows, arms and shoulders? They're probably working much harder than they need. Let them go a bit – they'll work much better without so much effort and interference.

If you don't remember to do all this before the first corner, fine; the thing to realise is that driving is a wonderful opportunity to put your lessons into practice. Become more aware of what you are doing. Stop. Put your new Directions into practice and you'll find you break that vicious circle of stress and excess muscle tension leading to yet more stress.

Golf

AIR VICE-MARSHAL DAVID CLARK CBE, Alexander Teacher

Golf is one of the most difficult of games. The terrain, the opponent, the technical problems of delivering a precise blow to a small ball with a variety of purpose-built instruments call upon sufficient skills and aptitudes to tax even the most resourceful of players. However, by far the greatest problem that any golfer faces is himself. A golfer who wishes to excel, or even just to play well enough to satisfy the demon lurking in each one of us, is faced with the question – how should he use himself to achieve the best performance of which his body and mind are capable, without causing damage to himself in the process?

I have been playing golf for more than 40 years and achieved my lowest handicap of six when I was in my fifties, but the greatest improvement in my play and understanding of the golf swing came after training as an Alexander teacher in my sixties. The reader may find this only to be expected after devoting some three years to improving my kinaesthetic sense and powers of direction. However I would be less than honest if I did not confess that at the time it seemed neither easy nor inevitable. The improvement was not the result of more practice or instruction on the technical side of the game. If anything it came from a lesson I was given by a very experienced Alexander teacher. Not being a golfer, he stuck to first principles and restricted his teaching to my thinking and my general approach to the game. He coached me in adopting a position of mechanical advantage when addressing the golf ball and worked to rid my mind of any trace of end-gaining when making the stroke. Simple as the instruction seemed, when I put it to the acid test on the golf course it worked at once and has continued to do so ever since.

The answer to becoming a better golfer lies in the individual accepting as his own the responsibility for developing an ability to employ the principles of the Alexander Technique while on the golf course. The advice and guidance of an Alexander teacher will make the task very much easier. Happy golfing!

Occupational therapy

NICOLA GOLDSMITH   Senior Occupational Therapist, Mount Vernon Hospital, Plastic Surgery Unit

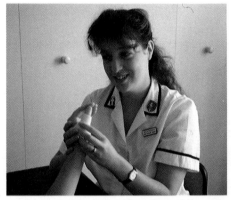

Occupational therapists work in all fields of health care to promote independence in daily activity for any person with a physical, psychological or social dysfunction. I work in a plastic surgery and burns unit, primarily with people who have had hand surgery. This particular speciality appealed to me initially because I was so affected by back pain that I was unable to apply for jobs involving lifting. Two years ago, before I discovered the Alexander Technique, I had a standing tolerance of about 10 minutes and found a 45 minute ward round almost impossible without the aid of either a corset or a TENS machine. My quality of life was dreadful; I was unable to carry even light loads like a baby or my cat and just the thought of going to the supermarket had me reaching for pain-killers.

Then came the enlightenment; I started to take Alexander Technique lessons.

In the early days, I remember a significant increase in pain around my neck as I tried to alter my appalling posture. In order to give myself a sense of achievement I set myself tiny goals – but it was a slow process. I had developed so many bad habits, holding the pain tightly located in my back and never allowing it to move. My Alexander teacher was wonderful; she encouraged me throughout and assured me there would be an end, and sure enough, within a year I felt so much more able to cope. I could sleep through a whole night, walk to the letter-box and breathe and position myself through the bad times. I have achieved so much and now feel able to attempt a return to my favourite hobby, abandoned seven years ago, badminton. Most importantly, I am no longer a person ruled by a bad back – I control it, it doesn't control me.

Most of my job tasks involve interacting with individuals and making hand splints or using activities and computers to promote function. The Alexander Technique has taught me to position myself and my patients in such a way that I am not putting any strain on my back, while still getting the best possible function from my patients.

Painting and drawing

GEORGE J D BRUCE   President of the Royal Society of Portrait Painters

An artist working in the great classical tradition which has continued for nearly 1,000 years has to have a basic training in drawing, design, tone, texture and colour relationships. Without such training, it is impossible for work to be carried out on a truly rational basis. If a painting runs into difficulties during its development, the artist's training will indicate that the difficulties can usually be put down to one of the above five. It is precisely when such difficulties do appear that the value of an Alexander-trained mind will come to the fore. A painter who has had Alexander lessons will more easily be able to keep the whole project under dispassionate review and he will more easily be able to observe deviations which may distract from the total forward progression of the work.

Drawing is not the ability to make straight lines or perfect circles freehand but an expression on a flat surface of forms and their related axes, actions and interactions with one another in three dimensional space. In talking of such actions of forms in space, we have a definite affinity between 'drawing' and the Alexander concept of 'Directing'. Both are concerned with relative axes, actions and interactions and positions of the whole sum of the human form. The Alexander Directions are concerned with the relativity in space of a part or parts of the structure of the body, one to another, and the direction for these to take up (e.g. lengthening and widening the back).

A continual appreciation of the principles of the Alexander Technique has affected my work by allowing me better use of myself, a clearer mind and continuing development of my perception of the world around me.

Playing an instrument

GERARD GRENNELL   Alexander Teacher, Professional Guitarist and
Musical Director

When I first heard about the Alexander Technique, it was already more than a year since my career as a professional guitarist had come to a sudden end. Needless to say, having found it virtually impossible to use my left hand without experiencing severe pain, I consulted every available specialist known to me, including alternative therapists, but without success.

So by this time, I was understandably more inclined to accept the situation as it was, rather than have my hopes dashed yet again by further attempts at a solution. However, the genuine concern of a few people whose experience of the Technique convinced me it was worth following up was valued when, to my astonishment, I was playing my guitar within weeks of my first visit. Then gradually, as the lessons progressed, so my playing improved, until eight months later I gave my first solo recital in two years.

During each lesson, my attention was drawn to the question of balance and how my perception of it had been altered by my reliance on habit. I was also helped to experience how, by being more in balance, it was then possible to improve my condition. So without needing to be told precisely how to play the guitar more efficiently, I could easily recognise when I was not.

By the time I was in a position to play without fear of interruption, my technique had changed so much for the better, that one would have been forgiven for thinking that I had been coached by a highly experienced guitar teacher. I am indebted to my Alexander teacher and the Technique, without which I would never have found an answer.

Public Speaking

CHRISTINA SHEWELL   Voice Teacher, Voice Therapist, Lecturer at the National College of Speech Sciences

In the average-sized house, there is seldom any difficulty in hearing the cries of a tiny baby. A small child utilises all the energy and spaces of his body to empower and amplify his voice. But as we grow older, our holdings, clenchings, slumpings and imbalances restrict the strength and distort the quality of our voices, and this is usually worse when we are nervous. As Alexander himself discovered, the voice cannot flow freely unless there is musculo skeletal balance within the body, for the body is the housing for the whole vocal instrument.

Our voices link our inner world of thoughts and feelings to the outer world of listeners, and if a speaker is tight with nervous tension, this will often be betrayed in the body. In my work to heal, develop and strengthen the voices of those who wish to speak, act or sing in the public arena, aspects of the Alexander Technique will always be incorporated. Releasing a clenched jaw will allow a warmer, more confident-sounding voice to stream out. Relaxing tense abdominal muscles so the breath can centre low in the body will give a strong base to a voice, and re-balancing a slumped head and neck will enable the larynx to be open, so that the voice quality is free and true. This natural, open quality is that which is needed for all those who wish to develop their voices in performance, in meeting the demands of their work, or simply to give confidence in personal conversation.

Riding

WALTER CARRINGTON   Alexander Teacher, Director of the
Constructive Teaching Centre Ltd, London

The Alexander Technique can be of great help to riders, as to
performers of all practical skills. It has been called a 'pre-technique' and
if beginners learn it before they sit on a horse, they will not only be taught
more easily, but more safely and will acquire a deep, safe, well-balanced
seat. This will enable them to use themselves effectively in the saddle to
give the aids and also to move in harmony with the horse, instead of
being an encumberance to it, as is so often the case.

On a personal note, I have found the Technique invaluable in
connection with my own riding, as have a great many Alexander teachers
and professional riding instructors. There is now a rapidly growing
interest in the Technique amongst those concerned with all branches of
equitation but especially amongst those concerned with the instruction of
beginners.

Most of us attempt to do new things in our old bad ways as far as poise
and balance are concerned. To protect our postural mechanisms from
habitual interference we should learn and practise Alexander's
Technique of 'conscious inhibition and direction', to 'think what we are
doing' in the true sense. As far as riding is concerned, initial practice on a
wooden saddle-horse is to be recommended, followed by work at a walk
on a live horse (on the lunge) where conscious activity is limited to the
primary orders on the part of the rider and the teacher can take care of
everything else.

Running

PAUL COLLINS   Alexander Teacher and Olympic Marathon Record Holder

I call it 'Alexander and the Art of Running'. Or should it be 'Running and the Art of Alexander'? At any rate, this art lies in the observation of one's running style, estimating its efficiency and sorting out modifications where needed. But the very same habit that makes a runner inefficient and prone to injury prevents him from making the changes needed.

To begin with, he can't see himself straight. My job as the runner's Alexander teacher is to give a helping hand in this; after all, it's much easier to spot what the other person's getting up to!

Put as simply as possible, good running consists in maximising the force taking you forward, while minimising any force taking you back. Obvious? But not applied by most runners. Like Alexander, I'm looking first at the balance of the head, then at the support of the torso; most runners expect the legs to do the whole support job *and* run into the bargain.

Of equal importance is the freeing-up of the double spiral musculature as it turns and twists around the axis of the vertebral column. This involves working on the freedom of the pelvis and shoulder girdle, without which the body is locked in a vice and the runner becomes 'muscle-bound'.

The innermost spring to be set free is the larynx. The runner who fixes in that area fixes everything else, not least his whole mental outlook.

Quite a lot to think about! However, I find in my running classes that repetitive injuries disappear, times improve consistently and enjoyment replaces drudgery.

Singing

PROFESSOR LYNDON VAN DER PUMP   Professor of Singing, Royal
College of Music, London

One of the most quoted maxims of the eighteenth-century Italian
masters – in this case, the great castrato, Pacchiarotti – says, 'He who
knows how to breathe knows how to sing'. It has long been accepted by
every reputable singing teacher that the management of the breath is the
key to producing good sound that will maintain through a lifetime. The
problem is how to accomplish this one unnatural action in singing –
stopping the inhaled breath escaping without any control – and not get
into a state of bad muscular tension, particularly around the upper torso
and neck.

Most modern teachers use the 'diaphragm supply with rib regulator' as
a basis for this: my own suggestion to students is that, having used the
muscles of the ribcage principally to inhale the breath, they continue
endlessly to 'breathe in', thereby keeping the ribcage expanded, to be a
regulating influence over the activity of the diaphragm for breath
support. The Alexander principle of isolating necessary muscular
tension, thereby not involving adjacent unnecessary muscles, leaving
them relaxed, is the perfect answer in finding out how to accomplish this
fundamental task. Also, the Alexander Technique's basic Primary
Control, when achieved, is perfect for physically freeing the throat and
allowing the breathing apparatus to work efficiently, setting up the
correct circumstances for producing good, natural, resonant vocal sound.

In my 23 years at the Royal College of Music, nearly every one of my
students has been advised at our first meeting to put their name down for
Alexander lessons! It is the perfect starting-point for learning about the
physical facts of the art of singing and how to put them into practice.

T'ai Chi Ch'uan

ROBIN SIMMONS   Alexander Technique and T'ai Chi Teacher, Director of Business Alexander

T'ai Chi Ch'uan has been practised as a health exercise, meditation and self-defence regime for hundreds of years in China. The immensely slow, careful, sinuous, precise, delicate and highly aesthetic movement forms of T'ai Chi produce a centred, grounded, peaceful, strong yet supple state that is both physically and psychologically refreshing.

Although very ancient, T'ai Chi has many principles that find an echo in the work of F.M. Alexander. Lightness, alertness and ease of action coming from an upright body attitude with a poised head balance are all prerequisites of appropriate T'ai Chi practice. When working with a partner in T'ai Chi it is vital to adopt an attentive 'listening' and adaptive attitude in making contact in activity.

T'ai Chi produces its own unique effect, as does the Alexander Technique, yet there are close similarities that become obvious to anyone practising both. These similarities are found in the fundamental principles as well as in the qualities that are required to inform all actions so that a general improvement in a person's standard of health is brought about – which is a common aim.

The actions of T'ai Chi produce a strange empowering quality that is similarly brought about by Alexander lessons. Breathing is steadied and deepened and there is a feeling of integrated connectedness that is also shared by the two disciplines. Having practised both for more than 20 years I can state unreservedly that Alexander Technique and T'ai Chi Ch'uan are mutually supportive and beneficial.

Tennis

MICHAEL BROWN   Alexander Teacher

There was a time when a game of tennis meant a great deal of frustration with more time spent picking up balls than actually playing. Since applying the Alexander Technique to my game, this is now starting to be a thing of the past. With my growing sensitivity and improvement in the way I move, through the application of the Alexander Technique, I find that I am now more able to attend to both what is occurring on the court, e.g. the flight of the ball and my opponent's movements, and to my own state of balance and freedom of movement. This enables me to experience greater control of my strokes and positioning and to inhibit the conditions which once caused me to suffer from pain in the shoulder and lower back.

The greatest benefit has been in my understanding of how my thinking affects my actions. Whereas previously my concern in winning the point led me to being out of balance and rushing my shots, I now inhibit my overriding desire to win and consciously direct myself so that I remain more in the moment and in touch with the requirements of staying free and in balance. Although my intention is still to win the point, I am now more capable of giving equal attention to ensuring I am functioning in a manner that will enable me to stay balanced and pain-free and play the best stroke available to me. Judging by the results, this approach is not only working but has opened up the possibility of improving my performance beyond my past limitations.

QUESTIONS AND ANSWERS

How do I find an Alexander Teacher?
The Society of Teachers of the Alexander Technique (STAT) lists
qualified teachers in the United Kingdom. These lists are available from
STAT (address at back of book). Please send a stamped, self-addressed
envelope.

Are all the teachers in STAT qualified professionals?
Yes. The training course duration is three years (1600 hours) leading to a
final certificate. Professional standards, which comprise both the setting
of well-defined criteria of clinical competence and the adherence and
enforcement of ethical codes of conduct are observed. A register of
members is available to the public. The table on pages 84–85, taken from
the BMA's *Complementary Medicine: New Approaches to Good Practice*,
Oxford University Press, 1993, gives a summary of the organisation and
work of STAT.

Will my doctor refer me?
Increasingly, GPs are suggesting the Alexander Technique to
complement orthodox medical treatment. If your consultant
recommends the Technique as part of your treatment, you may make a
claim on your private health insurance policy.

What conditions can be treated?
The Alexander Technique can alleviate back pain, postural disorders,
whiplash, breathing problems, myalgia rheumatica, repetition strain
injury, hypertension, anxiety, stress, and other chronic conditions.

Where can I learn the Alexander Technique?
There are over 500 practising teachers all over the UK giving individual
lessons. In addition, many Local Authorities offer both day and evening
classes, usually in groups of about 10 students. You can also do courses at
health and fitness clubs, sports centres, pain clinics and some health
farms.

How long will it take me to learn the Technique?
We recommend a basic course of 30 lessons, spread over a period of 2–3
months. Your teacher will give you ways to continue helping yourself
between your lessons and after your course of lessons has finished.

Will I have to take lessons for the rest of my life?
No. The benefits of your lessons, which are about re-education, will
continue as an on-going process, increasing your sense of well-being. You
may, however, find a 'refresher' course helpful at some point.

Society of Teachers of the Alexander Technique

Section One: *Organization*

Functions of organization	Details		Council/committee structure	Premises	Company status	Register of members
	Number of staff					
Promoting teaching of Alexander Technique. Supervising standards of training. Maintaining and improving professional standards. Upholding the code of ethics dealing with infringements. Preventing exploitation by untrained people. Facilitating contact between the public and teachers. Facilitating contact between members. Encouraging research.	1 full-time administrator (paid). 1 part-time administrative assistant. 1 part-time office junior.		Council: Chairman, Treasurer, Secretary, and 6 Ordinary members elected at AGM. Sub-committees: Ethics, Industry, Medicine and Research, Publishing, Office administration and Trust Fund, Professional Development, Publicity, International Liaison, UK/EEC regulations.	Leased office.	Members' association.	Yes.

Section Two: *Practice*

Conditions treated	Methods	Patient's GP informed of treatment	Referral by GP	Concurrent treatment	Ethical code
Can alleviate back pain, postural disorders, whiplash injury, breathing problems, myalgia rheumatica, RSI, hypertension, anxiety, stress, and other chronic conditions.	Teaching psycho-physical awareness, the basic principles and practice of poise and neuro-muscular co-ordination: how to change the habits of a lifetime.	Pupils with medical conditions usually advised to see GP.	Occasionally and increasingly.	Yes. Complementary to orthodox therapy.	Yes.

Section Three: *Training and qualification*

Entry qualifications	Clinical training	Post-graduate training	Examination	Course duration	Qualification	Course approval	Medical input in training
Good general education, mature personality. Interview. Sufficient previous Alexander experience.	Not appropriate.	Regular post-graduate and professional and development courses.	Continuous practical and oral assessment. External moderation.	1600 hours (3 years). 80% practical.	Certificate.	By Society in London and by affiliated societies overseas.	Relevant Anatomy and Physiology.

Reproduced by permission of Oxford University Press.

How to lie down

- Find a quiet place with a dry, warm floor
- Place a book on the floor
- Carefully lower yourself down on to the floor
- Let your head rest on the book
- Bend your knees up
- Rest your hands on your waist
- Let your weight drop down through the back of the head, the shoulders, hips and the feet
- Gently breathe out and notice the natural intake of air
- Give yourself about 15 minutes a day to stop and lie down

How to get up

- Stretch your arm up with your hand pointing up to the ceiling
- Point the hand across your body
- Roll over on to your side
- Bring your hands and knees underneath your body
- Rest in this crawling position
- Slowly rock forwards and backwards

- Come back on to your heels
- Come up on to your knees
- Let the head lead and the body follow, until you are standing up

Sitting

- Before you sit, stop and think
- Let your neck be free
- Let your head nod forward
- Let your knees bend
- Let your hips go backwards
- Think of your back lengthening and widening
- Sit gently on the chair
- Come back into the upright position
- Think of your weight going down through your sitting bones
- Maintain the length of the spine

Applied Sitting: Writing at a desk, working at a computer, playing the piano

- Ensure your chair is the right height
- Lift your arms and place the backs of your hands down on the surface of the desk
- Try not to lift your shoulders
- Breathe out
- Turn your hands over so they are flat
- Let your fingers lengthen out
- Think of your shoulders, elbows and wrists as open tunnels
- Think of widening under your armpits
- Take your hands off the desk/keyboard
- Allow your arms to drop down to your sides
- Let your fingers point freely to the floor
- Try to take short breaks

Writing

- Place your hand palm down
- Flex your wrist backwards
- Place your first finger and thumb together
- Gently flex them
- Lightly pick up the pen
- Flex your fingers while holding the pen
- Place the tip of the pen on the paper

Walk Tall

- Let your neck be free
- Let your head go forward and up
- Let your back lengthen and widen
- Stand equally on your feet
- Let your heel come off the ground
- Lift your foot
- Take a small step backwards

- Keep thinking of lengthening
- Let your foot go forward
- Transfer your weight forward on to this foot
- Try not to fall forward
- Keep an even, gliding rhythm

Whispered 'AH'

- Gently blow the air out through your mouth
- Do not move your upper chest and shoulders too much
- Close your mouth – let air come in through your nose
- Try not to sniff
- Allow your head to nod gently forward
- Think of something funny which makes you smile
- Allow your tongue to lie in the floor of your mouth, with the tip against the back of your lower teeth
- Let your jaw fall open
- Whisper a soft, open, easy 'AH'
- Shut your mouth
- Allow the air in through your nose
- Do about five 'AH's in succession
- Use a mirror if you find it helpful

Crawling

- Carefully lower yourself on to your knees one at a time
- Bend forward from your hips
- Have your hands directly underneath your shoulders and your knees underneath your hips
- Rock gently forwards and backwards
- Turn your head to the side and look at your hand

- Move that hand forward and at the same time move the opposite knee forward
- Turn your head back to the centre
- Turn your head to the other side and look at your hand
- Move that hand forward and at the same time move the other knee forward
- Repeat this pattern
- Let your head lead your body in a smooth movement

Squatting

- Stand with your head going forward and up
- Think of lengthening and widening along your back
- Have your feet apart
- Let your head pivot forward
- Keep your heels on the floor
- Let your ankles bend
- Let your knees bend
- Let your hips move backwards
- Try not to curve your spine
- Keep lengthening as you drop down

Bending and Lifting

- Place your feet apart with equal weight on your feet

- Let your neck be free

- Let your head go forward and up

- Let your back lengthen and widen

- Breathe out as you bend

- Let your head move forward

- Let your ankles bend

- Let your knees bend

- Let your hips move backwards

- Remember not to slump forward

- Think of your joints as supple and free

- To counterbalance the weight of the object you are lifting, allow your own body weight to go back and down through your heels